# First Picture Dictionary
## Animals

# Primer diccionario ilustrado
## Animales

**Pig**
*Cerdo*

**Butterfly**
*Mariposa*

**Rabbit**
*Conejo*

**Fox**
*Zorro*

Illustrated by Anna Ivanir

www.kidkiddos.com
Copyright ©2025 by KidKiddos Books Ltd.
support@kidkiddos.com

All rights reserved. No part of this book may be reproduced in any form or by any electronic or mechanical means, including information storage and retrieval systems, without written permission from the publisher, except in the case of a reviewer, who may quote brief passages embodied in critical articles or in a review.
First edition, 2025

**Library and Archives Canada Cataloguing in Publication**
First Picture Dictionary - Animals (English Spanish Bilingual edition)
ISBN: 978-1-83416-255-3 paperback
ISBN: 978-1-83416-256-0 hardcover
ISBN: 978-1-83416-254-6 eBook

# Wild Animals
## Animales salvajes

Lion
*León*

Tiger
*Tigre*

Giraffe
*Jirafa*

✦ *A giraffe is the tallest animal on land.*
✦ *Una jirafa es el animal terrestre más alto.*

Elephant
*Elefante*

Monkey
*Mono*

# Wild Animals
## Animales salvajes

Hippopotamus
*Hipopótamo*

Panda
*Panda*

Fox
*Zorro*

Rhino
*Rinoceronte*

Deer
*Ciervo*

### Moose
*Alce*

### Wolf
*Lobo*

✦ A moose is a great swimmer and can dive underwater to eat plants!

✦ ¡Un alce es un gran nadador y puede bucear para comer plantas!

### Squirrel
*Ardilla*

### Koala
*Koala*

✦ A squirrel hides nuts for winter, but sometimes forgets where it put them!

✦ ¡Una ardilla esconde nueces para el invierno, pero a veces olvida dónde las puso!

### Gorilla
*Gorila*

# Pets
## Mascotas

Canary
*Canario*

✦ A frog can breathe through its skin as well as its lungs!
✦ ¡Una rana puede respirar por la piel y por los pulmones!

Guinea Pig
*Cuy*

Frog
*Rana*

Hamster
*Hámster*

**Goldfish**
*Pez dorado*

**Dog**
*Perro*

◆ *Some parrots can copy words and even laugh like a human!*
◆ *¡Algunos loros pueden copiar palabras e incluso reírse como los humanos!*

**Cat**
*Gato*

**Parrot**
*Loro*

# Animals at the Farm
## Animales de la granja

Cow
*Vaca*

Chicken
*Gallina*

Duck
*Pato*

Sheep
*Oveja*

Horse
*Caballo*

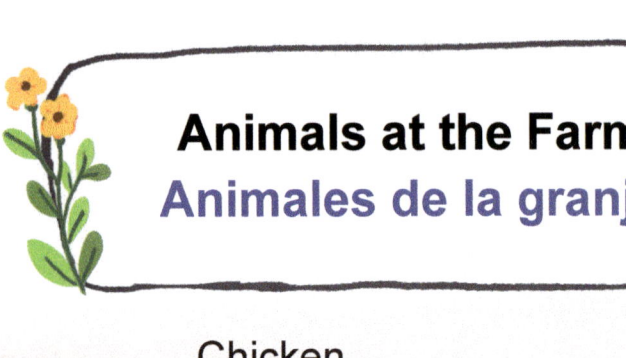

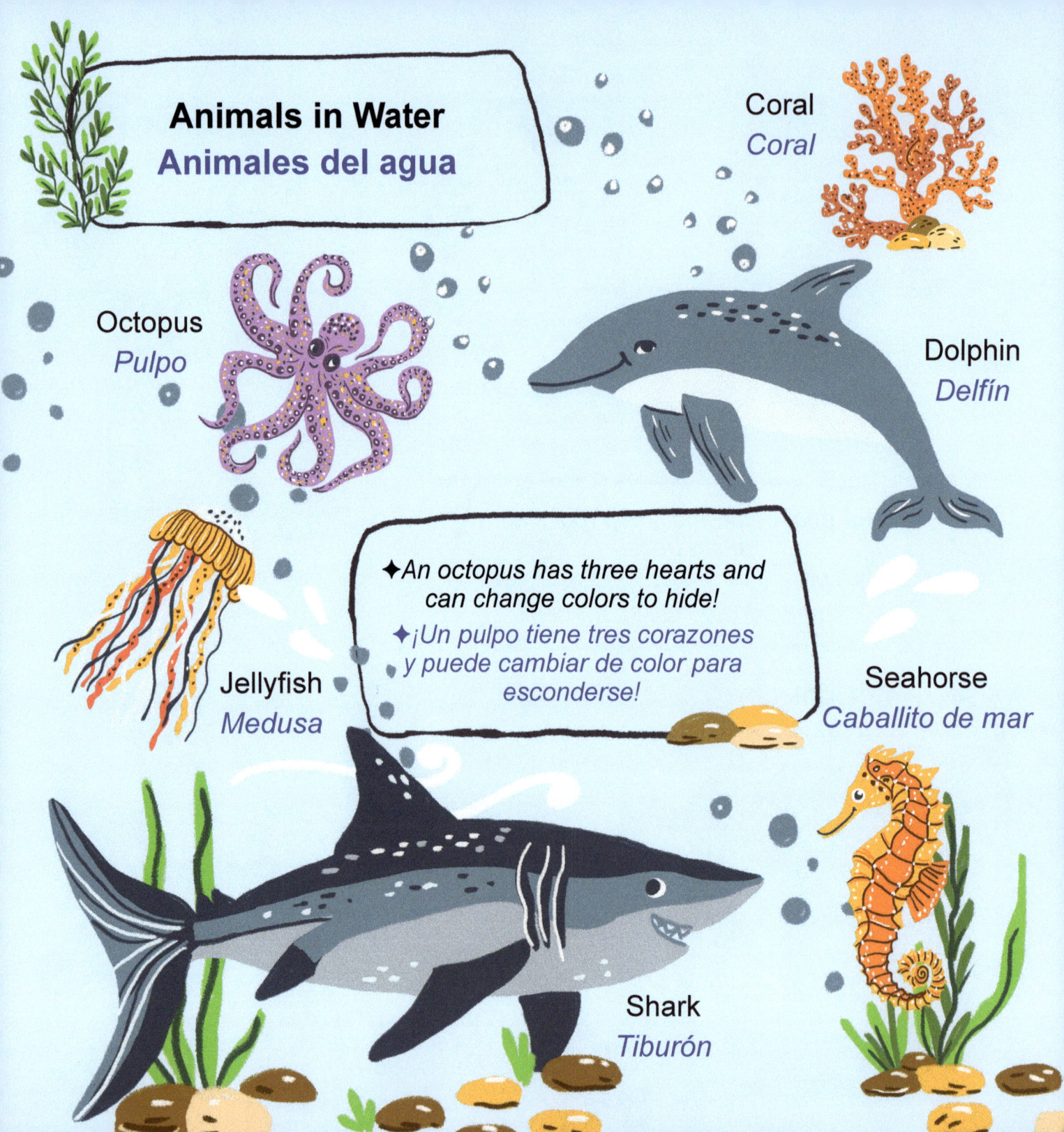

**Mosquito**
*Mosquito*

**Dragonfly**
*Libélula*

✦ *A dragonfly was one of the first insects on Earth, even before dinosaurs!*
✦ *¡Una libélula es uno de los insectos más antiguos de la Tierra, incluso anteriores a los dinosaurios!*

**Bee**
*Abeja*

**Butterfly**
*Mariposa*

**Ladybug**
*Mariquita*

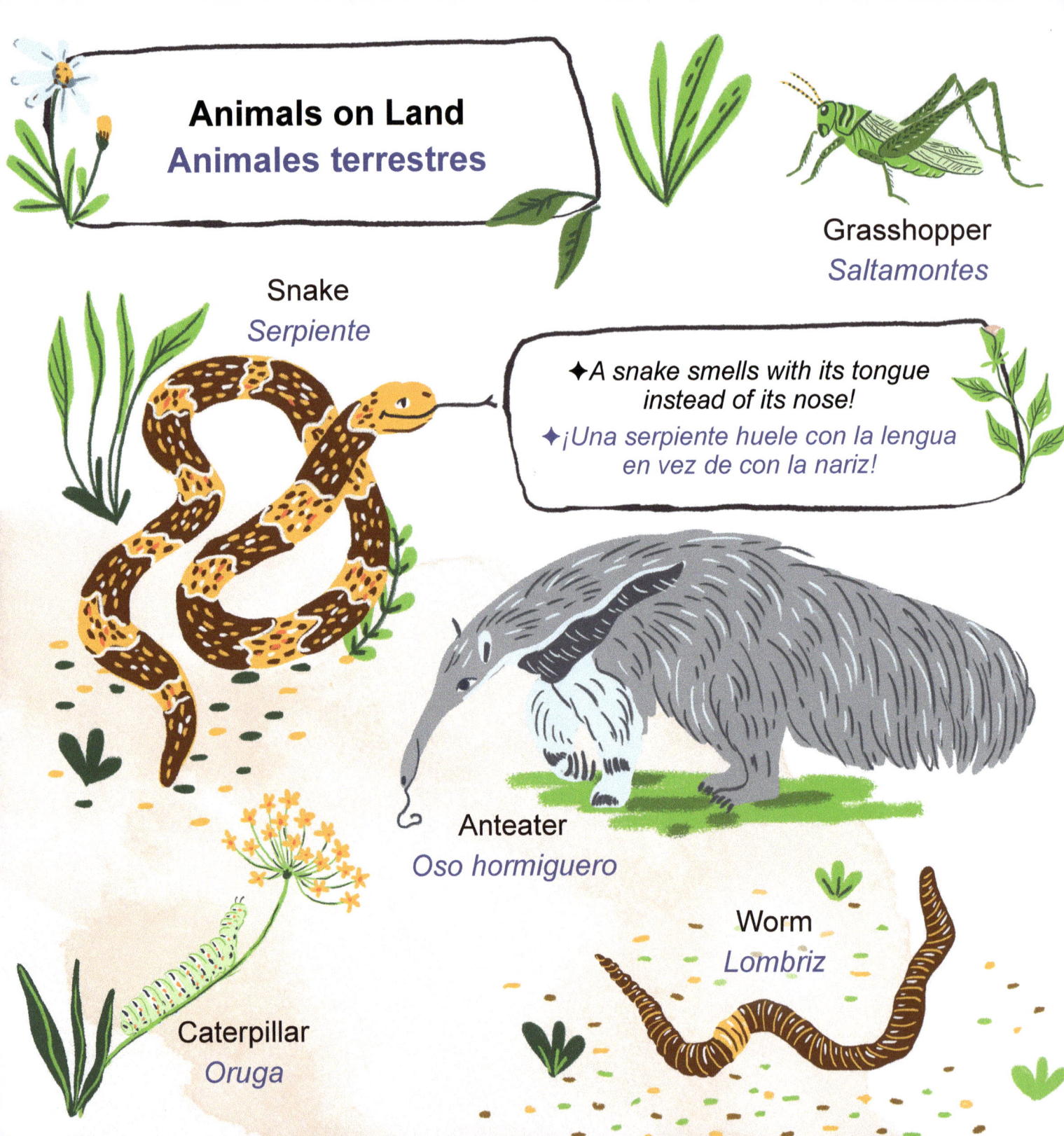

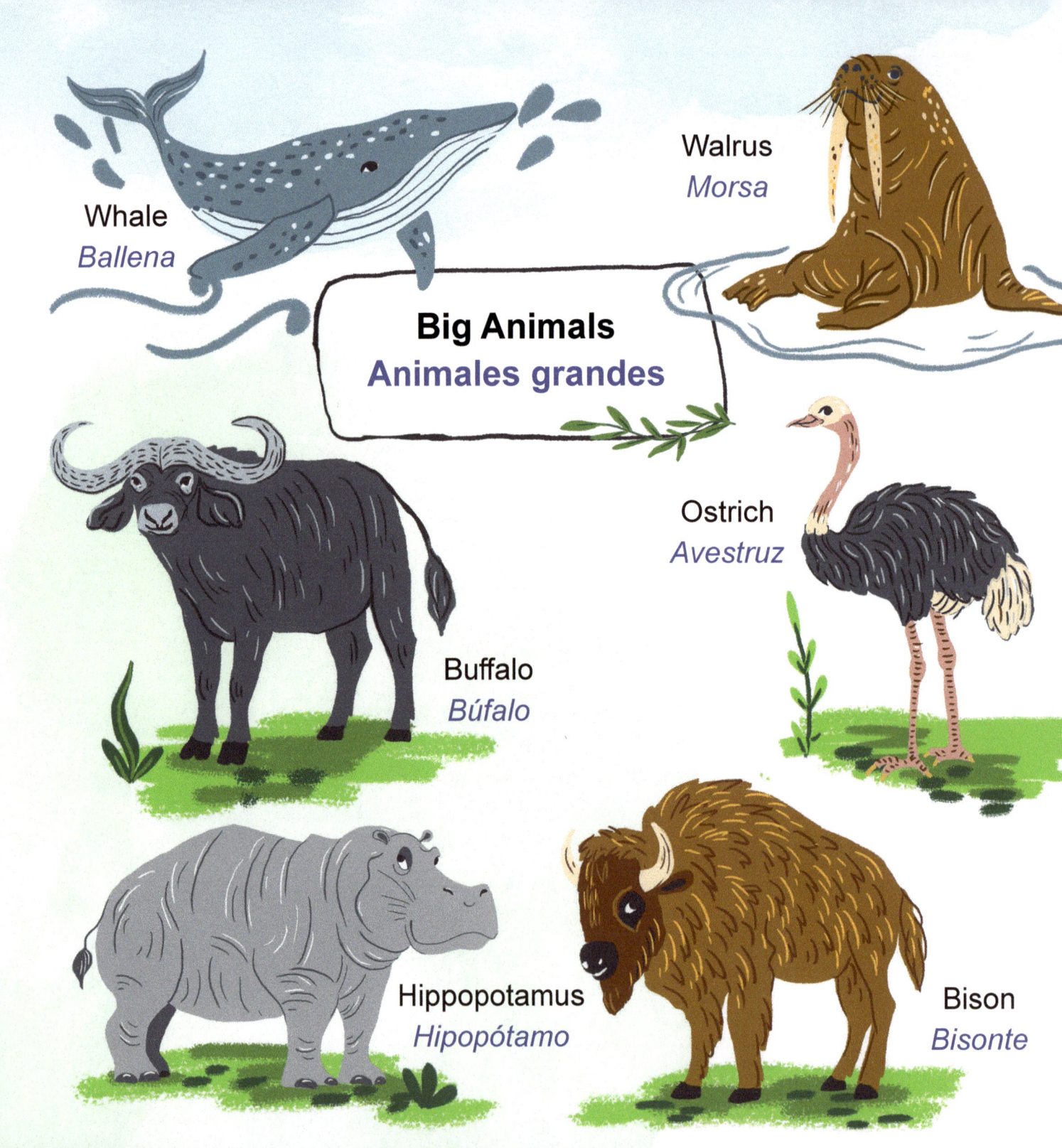

# Small Animals
## Animales pequeños

Chameleon
*Camaleón*

Spider
*Araña*

✦ An ostrich is the biggest bird, but it cannot fly!
✦ ¡Un avestruz es el ave más grande, pero no puede volar!

Bee
*Abeja*

✦ A snail carries its home on its back and moves very slowly.
✦ Un caracol lleva su casa en la espalda y se mueve muy lentamente.

Snail
*Caracol*

Mouse
*Ratón*

# Quiet Animals
## Animales silenciosos

**Ladybug**
*Mariquita*

**Turtle**
*Tortuga*

✦ A turtle can live both on land and in water.

✦ *Una tortuga puede vivir en la tierra y en el agua.*

**Fish**
*Pez*

**Lizard**
*Lagartija*

Owl
*Búho*

Bat
*Murciélago*

✦An owl hunts at night and uses its hearing to find food!
✦*Un búho caza de noche y usa el oído para encontrar su comida!*

✦A firefly glows at night to find other fireflies.
✦*Una luciérnaga brilla en la noche para encontrar otras luciérnagas.*

Raccoon
*Mapache*

Tarantula
*Tarántula*

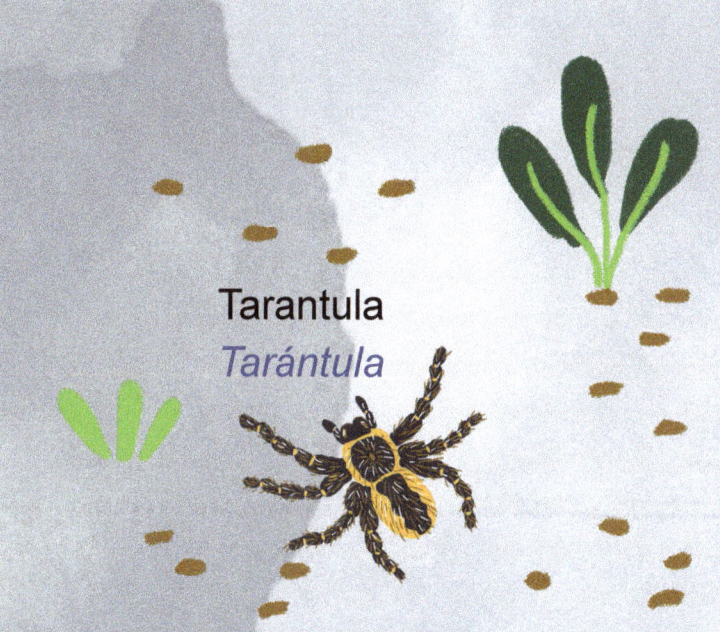

# Colorful Animals
## Animales coloridos

A flamingo is pink
*El flamenco es rosa*

An owl is brown
*El búho es marrón*

A swan is white
*El cisne es blanco*

An octopus is purple
*El pulpo es morado*

A frog is green
*La rana es verde*

✦ A frog is green, so it can hide among the leaves.
✦ *Una rana es verde, entonces puede esconderse entre las hojas.*

# Animals and Their Babies
## Animales y sus crías

**Cow and Calf**
*Vaca y Ternero*

**Cat and Kitten**
*Gato y Gatito*

**Chicken and Chick**
*Gallina y Pollito*

✦ A chick talks to its mother even before it hatches.
✦ *Un pollito habla con su mamá antes de nacer.*

**Dog and Puppy**
*Perro y Cachorro*

**Butterfly and Caterpillar**
*Mariposa y Oruga*

**Sheep and Lamb**
*Oveja y Cordero*

**Horse and Foal**
*Caballo y Potro*

**Pig and Piglet**
*Cerdo y Cerdito*

**Goat and Kid**
*Cabra y Cabrito*

www.ingramcontent.com/pod-product-compliance
Lightning Source LLC
LaVergne TN
LVHW072058060526
838200LV00061B/4768